THE OUT LIST

PORTRAITS BY TIMOTHY GREENFIELD-SANDERS
INTERVIEWS BY SAM MCCONNELL

INTRODUCTION BY RICHARD BLANCO

table of contents

foreword

ORLAN BOSTON

When I was asked to help create *The Out List* film and book, I didn't think twice about it. Never mind that I had never made a film nor published a book; I felt I had something to contribute. Working on this initiative would be one way of lending a hand to a cause that I feel passionately about: civil rights. It was an opportunity to help Timothy Greenfield-Sanders and his team tell the inspiring personal narratives of some of the most accomplished Americans alive today; real people leading real lives who just happen to be LGBT. This work, along with *The Black List* and *The Latino List,* is part of a larger collection of investigations by Greenfield-Sanders that explore race, diversity, accomplishment, and identity in America. Through intimate storytelling about love, family, military service, sports, politics, and the workplace, these portraits and stories illuminate the diverse tapestry of people that make up the changing face of who we are and who we are becoming as a society.

I am black, hispanic, and gay. I connected with this work and Greenfield-Sanders' past *List* projects on many levels. My parents have their own stories to tell and they were agents of social change by the example of the lives they continue to live. It wasn't so long ago that my white Spanish mother and my black father would have been prohibited from marrying under the law, with the forces against them using many of the same arguments being used today against marriage equality for LGBT Americans. In fact, interracial marriage only became legal five years before they met and seven years before I was born.

We've come a long way, haven't we?

As I write this, the place of the LGBT community in the United States is in a state of constant change. Change for gay men and women is everywhere, and these changes are not just profoundly important for members of the LGBT community, they are transformative of our society as a whole. Gay men and women now serve openly and proudly in the armed forces, enjoy the right to marry in over a dozen states (a list that is getting longer every year), and are in active dialogue with every aspect of our political system, from local legislative bodies to the United States Supreme Court.

Barack Obama spoke of LGBT rights in his second inaugural address, LGBT parents are becoming more common, LGBT youth are protected from bullying and discriminatory behavior, and the place of LGBT immigrants is seen as a legitimate consideration for our nation's immigration policy. And yet, despite all of this progress, it is still perfectly legal to be fired because you are LGBT. The rate of suicide for gay teens is five times that of their straight peers. Many transgender Americans still face widespread discrimination and hate crimes. And millions of hard working, taxpaying Americans are refused the benefits and protection under the law by being denied the right to marry.

The portraits in this book and in the film are as personal and intimate as the stories themselves. They depict the familiar and the unfamiliar. On one level these women and men are just like you and me. They are writers, editors, actors, musicians, law enforcement officers, financiers, comedians, politicians, fathers, mothers, athletes, teachers, and performers. But on a different level they have distinguished themselves by their commitment to change writ large—to the same kind of change my parents were willing to make on a more personal level in letting their love for each other triumph over the prejudices and biases that sadly linger in some dark corners to the present day.

You may label the characters in this book as you like: activists, reformers, dissidents, leaders, pioneers, or heroes. Each one is an agent of social change. As a group they are individuals who have overcome adversity, achieved success, and are now lending their voices for the fight for full equality.

They are Americans.

No minority in American history has made significant social progress without much help from Americans who number in the majority—in this case our straight ally brothers and sisters, people like Timothy Greenfield-Sanders and countless others. Without their help and support, the hands of time and change would surely count slower.

Let each of us find inspiration in all of these lives and now write our own stories.

introduction

RICHARD BLANCO

When I began writing this just a few weeks ago, I was in the closet. Let me explain: My partner Mark and I are staying at a guest house in Maine; we can't get wireless access to download the film preview of *The Out List Project* that Timothy had sent me so I could glean inspiration for these words. Luckily, we find the cable box in a walk-in closet; my handy husband fumbles with a few wires and—*presto*—he manages to connect directly to the Internet. We put the laptop on a shelf, sit on the floor, and lean back against the wall. He flops his leg over mine, and I start scratching his head in small, slow circles, just the way he likes it—force of habit after twelve years of marriage—as if we are in bed on a weeknight, not in a musty, dimly lit closet, again. Irony of ironies, I think as we watch and listen to the coming-out icons featured in this book, each one revealing their unique story of shame and fear, but also courage and triumph, always told with that tinge of campy humor and abiding love that are trademarks of survival. I begin connecting with their stories mirroring mine, not only through their words, which you will read in these pages, but also from the unspoken depth and sparkle of their eyes, the brush-stoke gestures of their hands, their crescent smiles, or closed lips when silence is all there is to tell, leaving only their very auras—like x-rays of the soul—that are captured in these brilliant portraits.

New York, April 2013

That night I take their words, their faces, and my notes on their lives upstairs with me. In the bedroom window the silver moon turns into a silver screen playing flash-back scenes of yet another closet: my mother's closet, the cave I'd hide in every time my grandmother scolded me for speaking too softly or painting my nails with crayons; every time she'd eye me eyeing the men's underwear ads and named me a fagot, wishing for another grandson. It was the safest place in the house, in the world. My world of mirrors, perfume sets, and silk scarves I'd dream of trying on, or choking myself with. Sometimes I'd carry Miso in with me—my cat, the only living thing that seemed capable of loving me back. Sometimes I'd reach for the photo albums on the top shelf and page through them scanning my own eyes in snapshots, wondering if there was ever a time when I was happy, not a defective little boy who loved all the wrong things. After a good, lonesome hour, I'd step out half-mended to brave the world and my grandmother's scorn again. But figuratively, I never left my mother's closet until I was twenty-five years old.

Flash-forward: I'm forty-five years old on a plane standing in line for the bathroom next to a middle-aged women with cropped silver hair wearing an FSU sweatshirt. She recognizes me and discretely asks in a half-whisper, "Are you the poet? The gay poet . . . from the inauguration?" I say, "Yes." Her eyes gloss over. "Thank you, thank you for what you did. It meant so much to us. Thank you," she says again. *Us*, meaning her, me, and also the spindly twenty-something boy sitting next to me reading a book of Rimbaud's poems. *Us*, the two Latino musclemen across the aisle sharing a blanket, their arms the size of my legs; and the Asian American man in the exit row wearing a burgundy sports coat and a pair funky of Prada glasses, watching Kathy Griffin on his iPad. *Us* meaning all of them and me, defined in the dictionary as people who exhibit sexual desire or behavior directed toward a person or persons of one's own sex. Vacuous words that reduce our lives to one-dimension, unable to contain the multiplicity and diversity of *us* jetting through the sky at thirty-thousand feet; or the *us* in the still-lives captured in these photos: sheriff, teacher, writer, and musician; politician, stock broker, actor, and comedian. And millions more from every imaginable walk of life, profession, and ethnicity.

There's no one word, no acronym, or definition that can do us justice. But is there a common experience we share that can begin to portray us more cohesively and intelligently? A multi-dimensional definition that can acknowledge our diversity while still connecting us in some fundamental way? Perhaps the answer lies in the very title of the book in your hands: *The Out List*. It evokes an experience we all share to some degree: that virtual closet each one of us lives in for some part of our lives; in some cases for most, if not all, of our lives; and tragically some who never make it out alive. Those invisible bars behind which we've all *done time*—from the days of Oscar Wilde to the founding mother-fathers of Stonewall, from the gay cowboys of the nineteenth century to the twentieth century lovers of *Brokeback Mountain*, from the murdered Matthew Shepard to the teenagers of today's queer-straight alliances. Although the circumstances and nuances of each closet experience are unique, the underlying emotional storylines are very similar, fraught with terror, loneliness, confusion, and isolation. But also hope, the light seeping in underneath the crack of the door we know we'll open someday when the time is right; or when times like the AIDS Crisis demanded it of us.

Stepping out (or stumbling out) of that proverbial closet is a rite of passage unique to us; it makes us a tribe defined and united emotionally and spiritually by the values such a rite instills in us, namely: a respect for diversity of all kinds, a desire to love others how we want to be loved, the courage to love ourselves, a commitment to justice and empathy for every underdog, and a desire to create and beautify the world, rather than destroy it. When we speak of *gaydar*, it's more than those obvious and cliché signifiers. We're picking up something more sublime, yet infinitely more powerful: those invisible scars and war paint on our faces; those tribal values tinted in our eyes that say to one another: *I have been where you have been, I know the darkness and the closed door, I have hurt as you have hurt, but I know the light, I am who you are, I believe what you believe.* Perhaps more than ever in our queer history, we ourselves are seeing ourselves not just through our sexuality, but into our very *humanality*. And it's contagious. America—indeed much of the world—has finally begun to value those values we uphold as a tribe, and coming to see them as transcendent and universal. Who can deny love, justice, equality without denying themselves of the same?

As I finish these words, I'm back in the closet again. Let me explain: I'm at my mother's house in Miami; and as I like to do every time I visit, I step back into her closet to remember my crying and her scarves, my loneliness and the scent of her perfumed soaps, my terror soothed by Miso's purring on my lap. But more so, I walk back in to say, *never again*. Ironically, it is the closet that keeps us out of the closet. The fear and sadness of ever having to live confined to that dank darkness again, keeps us fighting, picking the locks, breaking down new doors, and opening doors for others to step out and live and love as they were meant to and have the right to. Therein lies the importance of the words and people in these pages that are a testament and a picture book of our history; an artful manifesto; a travel log chronicling that journey out of the dark closet; a guidebook into the light.

STEPPING OUT (OR STUMBLING OUT) OF THAT PROVERBIAL CLOSET IS A RITE OF PASSAGE UNIQUE TO US; IT MAKES US A TRIBE DEFINED AND UNITED EMOTIONALLY AND SPIRITUALLY BY THE VALUES SUCH A RITE INSTILLS IN US . . .

Richard Blanco

neil patrick
HARRIS

actor/director

Neil Patrick Harris

Growing up, the fear of being gay was being effeminate. It was more about not being a man. I never felt sexually comfortable in my skin and that, I think, was exacerbated by the fact that I was not only recognizable, but had this very strange nickname everywhere I went. So, it made me less of a raconteur to be called "Doogie" and wear a bolo tie and glasses and be acne-ridden at The Standard.

Los Angeles, November 2012

I DON'T THINK THAT KIDS NEED A FATHER AND A MOTHER NECESSARILY. I THINK THEY NEED MALE AND FEMALE ROLE MODELS. BUT I DON'T THINK THAT MEANS THAT WE SHOULDN'T HAVE KIDS BECAUSE WE'RE TWO GUYS.

was in Rent, with this incredibly diverse gaggle of people. Gay guys that are like, "Fuck you, this is who I am, snap, snap." And straight guys that were super okay with gay people. And gay people that were super not okay with straight people. And that opened my eyes a lot.

I thought, oh wow, you can, kind of, be who you are and let the chips fall where they may. I wasn't really conscious of, "Oh my God, if I come out, I'll never work again." I just wanted to make sure that I presented myself in a way that allowed me the most opportunity to work.

I do think that it's difficult for someone who's got a sibilant "S", even if they're really masculine, if they're talking with a hardcore lisp, it's hard for them to be the football quarterback in a movie. I got on a TV show, *How I Met Your Mother*, and I thought, "Oh, that's interesting because I'm playing a very, very overt heterosexual on that show."

Perez Hilton asked my then-publicist whether I was gay. He was quoted as saying that "Neil's not of that persuasion." So, Perez started encouraging people who I had ever slept with to come forward and reveal themselves. And once that happened, I was like, "Oh, shit." So, we crafted a statement and said, "Yeah, here it is. I'm dating a guy and I'm proud to be gay." And then, we pressed send, and I was like, "Oh, God, what's gonna happen?" And then, nothing really happened. I assumed people would be more surprised than they were. Maybe I'm just super gay and everyone was like, "It's about time."

I met David Burtka in New York. I was walking down the street one day and a friend, Kate Reinders, is with this James Dean-y lookin' dude. I was like, "Kate. Nice job on this one." And she's like, "David? Oh, no, he's totally gay." And I said, "Really?" We started dating very quickly, actually. And, like a nice lesbian couple, moved in after, like, three months. We sort of have never been apart.

Neil Patrick Harris

I don't think that kids need a father and a mother necessarily. I think they need male and female role models. But I don't think that means that we shouldn't have kids because we're two guys. We don't encourage our child to only play with Barbies. But if our son picks up a Barbie doll and wants to play with it, okay. Parents need to be more accepting of who their kids are, and less concerned about who society thinks they need to be.

Growing up, I performed for my family, made my poor brother learn "It's a Hard Knock Life," and we'd dance around with brooms. It's such an interesting time now, I think, because the gay visibility is so prevalent. Parents of *Annie*-singing seven-year-olds would be more conscious that maybe their son might grow up to be gay. And I really, legitimately feel my parents never were aware in that way, or nervous of it, or even quite contemplated it. Now, there are so many examples of "gay" that you can't just put the gay in the little gay box anymore. You can watch *The Amazing Race* and see a gay couple fight, argue, and win. General, normal, mainstream Middle America, that doesn't get out and witness a lot of diversity, I feel like they get that diversity through television.

Who you sleep with is who you sleep with. It's really how you behave as a human being and how you treat others that speaks to your character.

WHO YOU SLEEP WITH IS WHO YOU SLEEP WITH. IT'S REALLY HOW YOU BEHAVE AS A HUMAN BEING AND HOW YOU TREAT OTHERS THAT SPEAKS TO YOUR CHARACTER.

Neil Patrick Harris

janet
MOCK

writer/activist

Janet Mock

I was kind of a dreamer growing up. I would just write about when I would have long hair, write about laying in the grass and talking to a boy and doing things that I think my peers took for granted. So, I always knew that I would be a writer in New York City, telling stories, as a woman.

New York City, September 2011

was named after my father. His name was Charles. I was his first son. I was his namesake. And I think that always frustrated him a bit, 'cause he wanted his son to be very tough.

I can't remember a time when I didn't know that I was a girl, wanting to always be in the kitchen with my aunts and my grandmother, and hearing them talk about the world and talk about, you know, women's problems and gossiping about other women.

I didn't hear the term "transgender," "transsexual." I didn't know what "trans" was. And I remember in the seventh grade, coming up to my mother and telling her,

"Mom, I'm gay." Just like any other person, I confused gender and sexuality. But I quickly realized that, no, I was always meant to be a girl and I just happened to have the wrong equipment.

The transition process for me probably started out with Lip Smackers. And I had a necklace full of the different flavors of Lip Smackers. I'd put them on in class as a way of expressing myself as female. At the time, I didn't know that I was doing this, but now I look back and I'm like, "Oh my God, what was I doing?" But it was my

JUST LIKE ANY OTHER PERSON, I CONFUSED GENDER AND SEXUALITY. BUT I QUICKLY REALIZED THAT, NO, I WAS ALWAYS MEANT TO BE A GIRL AND I JUST HAPPENED TO HAVE THE WRONG EQUIPMENT.

Janet Mock

way of telling my peers, the people around me, that I'm taking these steps.

When puberty hit, I was a late bloomer. I could see a burgeoning Adam's apple and I could see a bit of peach fuzz. The reflection of myself that I'm seeing in the mirror doesn't look like the person that I've always seen myself as. I was so lucky and so blessed in the fact that I had support at home, and I started the process through my endocrinologist.

At 18, I had already fully transitioned. For trans people, the "T" in LGBT, I think there's a sense, inherently within us, that we want to blend in. After transitioning, I just wanted to live a normal life as just another girl in the crowd. But I think, after a while, I kind of felt as if I was hiding something. Around the time I started writing my memoir, I found out about the murder of Larry King. I saw myself in him—fighting every day, tryin' to figure out who you are. He didn't have the chance to live, and I was so blessed in my life. I had parents who loved me, and a family who loved me. And I had great teachers who believed in me. And I don't think that I had all of those things dropped into my life to live silently. I overcame all of those things for a reason. To tell kids that you are beautiful and that nothing is unusual or strange about you because you're gay or lesbian or transgender or gender-queer, however you want to express yourself. That nothing is wrong with you.

We've had many, many victories and celebrations for our gay brothers and lesbian sisters. But we can't ignore the fact that transgender people are casualties in this fight. The federal government does not protect us from discrimination when we're trying to apply for a job or keep our job.

I see kids who are transitioning. They're gonna grow up and be able to say, "I'm trans," just the same way that their gay and lesbian counterparts can say, "Yeah, I'm gay, I'm lesbian." I met a 14-year-old girl who told me that she wanted to be a writer like me someday. She didn't say she wanted to be as pretty as me. I knew she was transgender, but that's not what she connected with. She just connected with the writing. She had such a strong sense of self. "I want to be a writer like you someday."

WE'VE HAD MANY, MANY VICTORIES AND CELEBRATIONS FOR OUR GAY BROTHERS AND LESBIAN SISTERS. BUT WE CAN'T IGNORE THE FACT THAT TRANSGENDER PEOPLE ARE CASUALTIES IN THIS FIGHT.

Janet Mock

dustin lance
BLACK

screenwriter

Dustin Lance Black

I grew up in San Antonio, Texas. My family's military and Mormon. We'd go to church every single Sunday. One Sunday, they beamed in the president of the church, Spencer W. Kimball. And his message was that homosexuality is sin. I knew he was talking about me. And so, my first impression of my own sexuality, my own love, was that it was a sin comparable to murder.

Los Angeles, April 2011

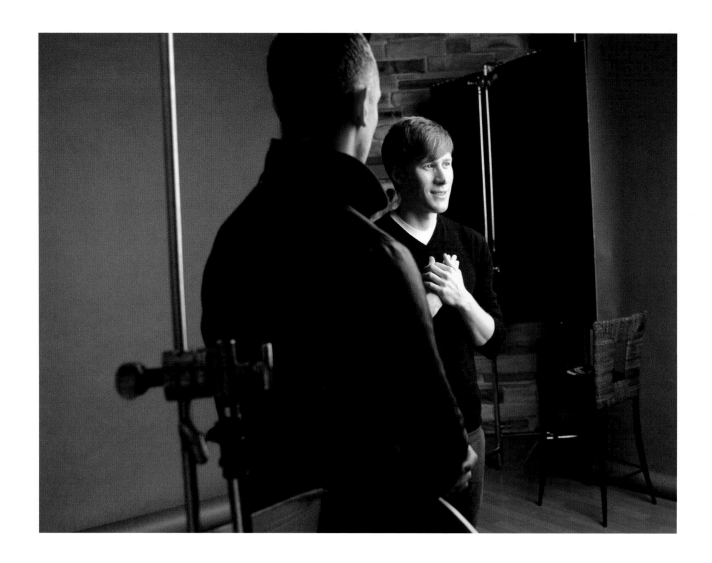

was a closeted gay kid in the '80s and I knew my sexuality. I was attracted to movies that were magical reality. One day, I went to the video store. I think I was 13. I saw a movie and I was like, "I have to have this movie." And this movie was called *The 400 Blows*, and it was not what I was hoping it would be at all. It was actually, you know, François Truffaut's masterpiece. And it was a film about a real family that was troubled, and a kid, and how he deals with it. I had no idea that cinema could be reflective of my own life. It did change me and it made me feel less alone in the world. And I thought, "Boy, I want to do something like that."

The time between realizing I was gay and coming out was about 15-16 years. I was probably 20-21 years old and I'd come home for Christmas, which is when it often happens. And my mom was sitting on my bed. We always did this—stay up and talk all night long. And she starts railing against "Don't Ask, Don't Tell." And it wasn't because it wasn't inclusive enough. It was because, how dare they allow gay people into the military? And she was really passionate about it. I wasn't ready to come out, but I started to cry. And she's a really sensitive, sweet mom. And she knew. She knew, right then and there. It was a quick conversation.

My mom is paralyzed from polio. She knows what it's like to be different and to be judged for being different. She showed up to the Academy Awards wearing a white marriage equality ribbon.

I have heard some filmmakers say they don't want to be labeled as a gay filmmaker. I am a gay filmmaker. I'm a gay guy. I'm not ashamed of that. I'm pretty proud of that, in fact. And also, the truth is, being gay in America today certainly influences who you are and how you see the world. And that's my voice. Being a gay filmmaker helps you see other people and their differences, and to have empathy for what their differences do to their character. I'm not gonna run from that label.

In 2008, I campaigned for Obama in Nevada and in Virginia. It was thrilling to see him get up there and to give that speech on election night, a speech where he said the words "gay" and "lesbian," and that we were a part of this new vision. But then, I went on the laptop and just started refreshing the results coming in on Prop 8 and it became increasingly clear we weren't gonna make it. That, in California, we were left out of the dream.

I HAVE HEARD SOME FILMMAKERS SAY THEY DON'T WANT TO BE LABELED AS A GAY FILMMAKER. I AM A GAY FILMMAKER. I'M A GAY GUY. I'M NOT ASHAMED OF THAT. I'M PRETTY PROUD OF THAT, IN FACT.

I just remember thinking, boy, you know, what about that kid out there in San Antonio, Texas, right now, who tunes in and sees the next day that gay and lesbian people had their rights stripped away in California? They're still second-class, they're still less-than. And I know all too well the dire solutions that may have flashed through that kid's head. Those messages are dangerous. I think that that election result cost lives. I do. So, I was heartbroken.

Every day that we don't have full equality, every day that those messages are still being sent, that gay and lesbian people are second-class in this country, the result is that more gay and lesbian kids are getting bullied. And my hope is that we win this fight much faster than many think we can. I wanna be out of the business of civil rights fighting as soon as possible.

Dustin Lance Black

lupe
VALDEZ

sheriff

Lupe Valdez

I grew up in San Antonio, where everybody lived in certain areas. The Hispanics lived over here. The Anglos lived over there. The African Americans lived over there. In order for me to go to college, somebody said, "You have to bus yourself across town to go to those better high schools." It took me a while to realize why I was the only one with dirty shoes when it rained. The other neighborhoods had sidewalks and paved streets while our *barrio* did not. That was the first realization that we were different.

New York City, July 2012

n college, I tried to date guys. But they were, like, buddies. People said, "You have to date." So, I would go on a date and enjoy myself, but it was the women that I was attracted to. It would've been very difficult for me to accept my sexuality had I not made the connection with spirituality.

I read an article about MCC (Metropolitan Community Church). And I, and just like every other person that ever tried to come in, drove around the church for a couple of times, trying to get brave enough to walk inside. I think I teared through the whole service.

At the end, they always served communion, and right in front of me, as we were lining up, was a gay couple with two little girls. And I guess I must have said it out loud, but I said, "Oh my God, where have you been?" And the woman right in front of me turned around and said, "We've been here, waiting for you." God made it possible for me to see that, to help me accept who I was.

In 2004, Dallas County was very Republican, very conservative. And here you have a female Hispanic lesbian

GOD MADE IT POSSIBLE FOR ME TO SEE THAT, TO HELP ME ACCEPT WHO I WAS.

Lupe Valdez

Democrat running for sheriff. In the primaries, I was the only woman. The rumor mill started going, "You know, we might have a woman sheriff. Yeah, we might have a lesbian sheriff." One of the state legislators gave me some very good advice. She said, "Don't let that be the first thing that comes out about you. Let them hear about your career and your standards and who you are."

In this neighborhood, I saw a sign: "Bush for President." And then, right next to it was a little sign that said, "Valdez for Sheriff." So, I said, "You know what, I may win." Dallas County was Republican but, in spite of that, they were able to see past the party lines, they were able to see past the sex lines—this person appears to be the best candidate.

After I got elected, I went to the Hispanic group and they said, "We got you elected." I went to the LGBT group and they said, "We got you elected." And I couldn't have done it without the support of different groups.

Right after I got elected, I got on a flight and somebody sat next to me who said, "Are you Lupe Valdez?" And I remember thinking, "Oh, no, here we go. Why is this woman talking to me? She's Anglo, she's well-to-do, and she's probably Republican." And then she says, "My son is gay." And I went, "Okay." And I said, "Tell me about your son." Well, he went to the high school where her husband coached. He was not out. And they were so scared that he was going commit suicide, because he was so depressed. "And how is your son now?" She said, "Oh, he's wonderful. He came out to us, and he and his partner live down the street from us. They go to college and, once a week, they come over and have a meal with us." She says, "I have to take your picture. My son will never believe that I sat next to you. With your election, you validated my son." You know, I wanted to scream, "Why can't we just get validated for being human beings and being who we are?" We need to make sure that it's okay to be who we are.

DALLAS COUNTY WAS REPUBLICAN BUT, IN SPITE OF THAT, THEY WERE ABLE TO SEE PAST THE PARTY LINES, THEY WERE ABLE TO SEE PAST THE SEX LINES—THIS PERSON APPEARS TO BE THE BEST CANDIDATE.

wade
DAVIS

athlete

Wade Davis

Sports was my life. I was the biggest Deion Sanders fan. I mean, I had a shrine in my room. I had life-size posters. I had about 50 Deion Sanders football cards. I was obsessed with Deion Sanders.

New York City, July 2012

I WAS A MAN'S MAN. I LIKED SPORTS. I
TALKED SHIT. EVERY MAN THAT I KNEW
THAT WAS PERCEIVED AS GAY SANG IN THE
CHOIR OR PLAYED WITH GIRLS. I DIDN'T DO
ANY OF THOSE THINGS, SO I HAD A HARD
TIME TRYING TO RECONCILE WHO I WAS
WITH WHO THEY WERE.

grew up very religious. I went to church probably three to four times a week. No one ever specifically ever told me that being gay was wrong, but I remember my family and friends just having some very negative conversations about people who they referred to as "bull daggers." I couldn't be that.

In the high school gym, there was a kid who I just couldn't take my eyes off of. No, I'm not gay. This is just a phase I'm going through. Every guy checks out other guys' bodies. It's a comparison thing. But then, I realized all my friends are talking about girls, but I cannot take my eyes off of this guy. I knew instantly that who I was was never going be accepted, whether it was in my family or on a football field or with my friends.

My dream was to play in the NFL. There was nothing that was going to stop me. The idea that I could be gay and a sports player just didn't match, because the image of a gay man was always effeminate. I deemed myself as masculine. I was a man's man. I liked sports. I talked shit. Every man that I knew that was perceived as gay sang in the choir or played with girls. I didn't do any of those things, so I had a hard time trying to reconcile who I was with who they were.

I was in the gym and this gentleman was doing a stupid machine called the Gravitron. He was everything I thought I wanted in a guy. He was straight-acting, he was totally passable, and he liked sports. We never had a discussion that we were dating or in a relationship. It was just one of those things where, one day, we were sitting in the car and our hands touched.

There was this budding relationship and then, because I had to go over to NFL Europe, I had to figure out a way to talk to him every day. I would literally have my teammates in the room, but I would refer to him as if he was a girl. I became the world's greatest liar. My first check was a couple thousand bucks, and I remember going to the strip club, blowing almost every penny of it, trying to make guys think that I was into these girls. I really worked as hard as I could to make sure that they thought I was one of them.

I was in a city called Sitges. And for those who know Sitges, it is the second highest gay-populated place in the world. I had no clue of that. I remember we arrived there, and I'm like, "There are a lot of men here in Speedos with their shirts off." And I was thinking to myself, "God is punishing me."

I had the worst year of my life playing over in Spain. I was angry. I just wanted to experience being gay for just five seconds, just to be able to talk to someone, to be able to . . . to kiss a man, and not have it be an issue. I felt as if that was one of the few times where I could've done that without being ostracized.

The friendship of my teammates was probably a bigger reason why I was afraid to come out. When you play a sport, you create a family. I never told anyone that I was gay until I stopped playing football. It's impossible to talk to your mother every single day and have this secret that she doesn't know about. And at that time, I had a partner of two years. And I was just sick of it. I was sick of the lies. He was sick of being called Stephanie, too. So, I flew home and we went for a walk. And I said, "Mom, I have something to tell you." And she said, "What?" like she had no clue. I was like, "I'm gay." And her first words were, "You know that's an abomination, don't you?" "I know . . . I know that's what you think." And her second thing she said was, "You're already black. I still love you and we'll work through this, but I just need time."

I thought about lying to her, saying, "I'm not gay, that was just a phase." Because I had been living with the pain and I seemed to be okay. I didn't want her to have to go through the same pain too, so I contemplated going back in the closet for a very long time.

I think if a major league player came out, it would really change the conversation of what it means to be a masculine man. If we wait around till every athlete says, "I'm fine with someone being gay," the world will end. I think that we have to just push the boundaries now.

Wade Davis

r. clarke
COOPER

log cabin republican

R. Clarke Cooper

It is much easier to be a gay man in the Republican Party than it is to be a Republican in the LGBT community. The LGBT community, which tends to be predominantly left-leaning politically, will say, "How do you deal? Oh my God, it must be such a burden. It must be such great pain to be moving in conservative circles." My 80-percent friend is not my 20-percent enemy. As a conservative, as a person of faith, I have more in common with fellow conservatives.

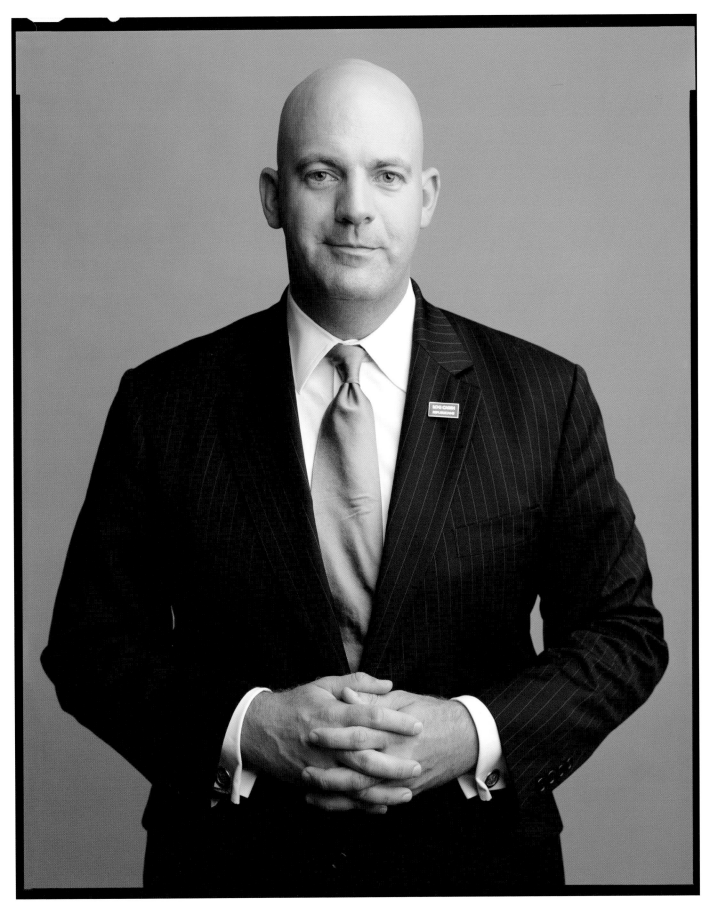

New York City, September 2012

I CAME TO
REALIZE THAT
MY ORIENTATION
IS A GIFT FROM
GOD, JUST AS
MUCH AS THE
ORIENTATION OF
MY HETEROSEXUAL
BROTHER IS HIS
GIFT FROM GOD.

Growing up in a place like Tallahassee, Florida, it was very much similar to earlier generations. We had sock hops, bonfires, white-tailed deer hunting. I was an Eagle Scout. Growing up, anybody that would be identified as gay would be . . . would fall into a certain stereotype: the man that did my mother's hair at the salon or the florist.

As a Christian, I spent a lot of time praying that being gay would go away. That said, I was very blessed to have a godparent, my Uncle Larry. My parents had to sit down and explain to us that Uncle Larry's roommate was actually his partner. So, very early on, I had, not a peer, not somebody that was a caricature, but a positive gay role model.

And, I do credit Uncle Larry to saving my life. I came to realize that my orientation is a gift from God, just as much as the orientation of my heterosexual brother is his gift from God.

The Log Cabin Republicans, we're the LGBT group of the Republican Party. Essentially, back in the late 1970s in California, there was a state proposal known as the Briggs Initiative, which would have banned gays and lesbians from teaching in public or state classrooms. A group of like-minded gay and lesbian Republican schoolteachers said, "We need to organize."

With the success of actually killing this potential state measure, the Log Cabin Republicans, at a very grassroots level, realized it is conservative to be supportive of the LGBT community and equality. The federal suit filed by Log Cabin Republicans that challenged the federal statute, "Don't Ask, Don't Tell," banning gays and lesbians from serving in the military, was initiated by Log Cabin Republicans. Yes, President Obama signed the bill. But we put that bill on his desk.

When I first took the job to run Log Cabin Republicans, one member of Congress from Texas asked me, "When did you become a gay?" We were having the conversation of, "Is it a choice? Is one's orientation a choice?" And that's when I realized not only how important our institutional role was, but also that it was incumbent upon us to educate lawmakers.

Society at large is moving in the direction of full recognition and equality for LGBT Americans. It's important that people come out. If family, friends, neighbors, and staff members come out, it's harder to ignore these issues when you are constantly reminded or surrounded by people, whom you respect and love, who happen to be L, G, B, or T.

R. Clarke Cooper

lady
BUNNY

drag performer

Lady Bunny

Drag pushes my adrenaline button. I love to go out in drag because you can make an entrance. You can go up to the cutest boy in the club and grab him by the crotch, which I would never dream of doing if I were not in drag. So, drag queens can get away with murder.

New York City, July 2012

The first time I was in drag, I was a snake charmer. I've charmed a few snakes since then. I was in love with *I Dream of Jeannie*, Barbara Eden. In the first-grade show, my mom made me that outfit and I wore cat-eye, you know, '60s eye makeup. Even though everyone knew that I was a sissy, somehow, I got over. I was just like, you know, somewhat loud-mouthed and extroverted and popular.

I was attending Georgia State. I became RuPaul's roommate. He and I were backup dancers for a group called the Now Explosion. He got us a gig and we headed up to New York. The club was drag queen owned and operated, but these were drag queens out of the mainstream. You really felt like you were part of a scene that was unique. Drag queens fronting bands like Tanya Ransom, or doing plays like Ethyl Eichelberger, or taking lip-synching and making it an art form, as Lypsinka did.

Wigstock was born one night when the Pyramid closed and we were not ready to stop drinking. Wendy Wild, Hattie Hathaway, and a bunch of others grabbed 40 ounces and went to Tompkins Square Park. We just thought of an idea to parody Woodstock with a festival of wigs and rock. I think the idea would have faded with the next day's hangover had I not actually sought out the permits. At its peak, we were getting maybe 30-45,000 people. Not just the performers came in costumes. There were amazing, creative people in New York at that time.

One of the big breakthroughs in drag was RuPaul's success. Because here,

BUT THE THING IS, I'M NOT TRYING TO BE A WOMAN. I'M USING WOMEN'S CLOTHING (IN RATHER LARGE SIZES) TO EXPRESS WHO I THINK I AM. THAT HAS NOTHING TO DO WITH A WOMAN. THIS IS ABOUT ME, AND HOW I WANT TO DRESS.

Lady Bunny

IT WAS NOT THE CONSERVATIVE GAYS THAT
PUT ON A PINK T-SHIRT OR A RAINBOW FLAG
ONE DAY A YEAR AND THEN WENT BACK TO
THEIR CLOSETED OFFICE JOBS. IT WAS THE
DRAG QUEENS AND THE STREET PEOPLE
THAT WERE GETTING THE HARASSMENT BY
THE POLICE WHO SAID, "UH-UH. ENOUGH.
HERE'S A BRICK IN YOUR FUCKING FACE."

for the first time, you had a drag queen who was saying, "I am gorgeous and I am glamorous." In *Some Like It Hot*, or Milton Berle, or *Mrs. Doubtfire*, or *Tootsie*, there's always an excuse for them to have to be hiding in drag. They don't want to do drag.

I never understand why feminists have a problem with drag queens. There are some things that drag queens do, like rub imaginary boobs, or portray, as I guess I do, a tacky woman. But the thing is, I'm not trying to be a woman. I'm using women's clothing (in rather large sizes) to express who I think I am. That has nothing to do with a woman. This is about me, and how I want to dress.

Do gay kids value their predecessors? No, I don't think that they do. Don't you ever discount the drag queens. I get so tired of these conservative gays always saying, "The leathermen and the drag queens, they don't represent our community." Well, we started your gay rights. It was not the conservative gays that put on a pink T-shirt or a rainbow flag one day a year and then went back to their closeted office jobs. It was the drag queens and the street people that were getting the harassment by the police who said, "Uh-uh. Enough. Here's a brick in your fucking face."

Lady Bunny

larry
KRAMER

playwright/activist

Larry Kramer

Everything changed in July 1981, with the announcement of what would be called AIDS. I helped to start two major organizations, Gay Men's Health Crisis and ACT UP. On the one hand, so many of our friends were dying. And on the other hand, we slowly had a small army of people who were working so very hard to save the rest of us. It was during that time that I realized, number one, how truly proud I am that I am a gay man, and how truly wonderful I think gay people are.

New York City, March 2012

found that, with AIDS, the *Times* wasn't writing about us. Nobody was writing about us. The mayor wasn't answering phone calls. It was awful. People would rush up to me and say, "Have you heard of anything? Is there anything coming along? I don't think I'm gonna be able to last much longer." For many years, there wasn't anything. And you had to say to them, somehow, "Hold on, hold on," and give each other hugs.

ACT UP made itself. We began every meeting by announcing who had died since the last meeting. And boy, if that wasn't enough to keep you going, I don't know what would be. The first meeting had two hundred people. The next meeting, we had three hundred.

We had a demonstration the following week on Wall Street. Several thousand showed up, and we were born.

Well, it got more radical as it went on. And we decided to have a protest at St. Patrick's. We had all been trained in civil disobedience. And it was very carefully choreographed, what we were going to do. Like all good actors, these guys and gals really got into their parts. They faced the altar and yelled, "Stop murdering us." Cardinal O'Connor was having a fit. And, we were crucified ourselves the next day

ANGER IS A WONDERFUL EMOTION, VERY CREATIVE IF YOU KNOW HOW TO DO IT.

Larry Kramer

AND OUR PEOPLE WERE SCARED. "WHAT ARE WE GONNA DO? THEY HATE US." AND I SAID, "NO, THEY DON'T. THEY'RE *AFRAID* OF US. THIS IS THE BEST THING WE HAVE EVER DONE . . . WE'RE HERE, WE HAVE VOICES, AND WE'RE GONNA FIGHT BACK."

and on. Every major network, every major newspaper said the most awful things about ACT UP—how terrible we were, destroying people's right to worship.

And our people were scared. "What are we gonna do? They hate us." And I said, "No, they don't. They're *afraid* of us. This is the best thing we have ever done. We're no longer just limp-wristed fairies. We're guys in jeans and Levi's and boots. We're here, we have voices, and we're gonna fight back." It made us, that action at St. Patrick's.

Every treatment for HIV that is out there is out there because of us. Not from the government, not from any politician, not from any drug company. We forced all of those things into being by our anger and our fear. And that's what anger can get you. You do not get more with honey than with vinegar. Anger is a wonderful emotion, very creative if you know how to do it.

As much as we achieved, I don't think we've achieved that much. We still don't have rights. People are still doing terrible things to us. Matthew Shepard still exists, in one form or another. This government, to which we pay taxes, gives us very little in return compared to what it gives straight people. This is wrong. And it bugs the shit out of me. We have so much more to do! And we are so capable of doing it! Why aren't we doing it?

I really truly felt that, for some reason, I've been spared to tell this story. Everybody I know is dead, all my friends. I shouldn't say "everyone," but almost. I'm still here. Okay, thank you, God. I don't believe in you, but thank you anyway. This is what I'm gonna do to pay back.

Larry Kramer

wanda
SYKES

comedian

Wanda Sykes

When I was young, I remember having a crush on a girl who had a crush on my brother. I looked up at her and I said, "You know, I wish I were a boy because then you would want to be my girlfriend." And she let go of my hand and she's like, "No, no, you're a girl and you like boys, and that's it, and don't ever say that again to anyone." I felt like something was wrong with me and that was the moment when I said, "Oh, ok, that's right, I like boys. Yeah, yeah, of course, yeah, I like boys."

New York City, January 2013

was living as a straight woman . . . I would say, you know, a good wife. When the marriage ended, for other reasons, it was . . . it was very liberating. Then something, like, went off, "Well I tried that. It didn't work out. Let's get some pussy!"

A lot of African American culture is embedded with the church. That's another reason why it took me so long to deal with my sexuality. I go by what I read from the Bible. And, as Jesus said, "Above all these things, love thy neighbor as thyself." It'd be very easy to love everyone if they were all like you. You make everybody different, and he's like, "This is gonna be the hardest shit for you all to do. Is to love each other. That's going to be the hardest thing." He's probably just sitting, laughing, just going, "I knew, I knew they was going to mess this up." Instead of saying what not to do, I try to live by what he says to do. Love, yeah.

When I came out, it wasn't planned at all. There was a national day of protest against the passage of Prop 8. I said, "Okay, where's the rally? We're going to go to the rally." And I did and in my speech I said, "Hey, you know, I, you know I got married and, um,

I'M A BLACK WOMAN, A CELEBRITY,
AND I'M OUT. IT WAS A BIG DEAL.
NO REGRETS.

I'm pissed." I get to the hotel and I'm turning on the TV and on CNN's scroll, it's: Comedian Wanda Sykes, "I'm proud to be gay." And I was like, oh, this is a big fucking deal. I'm a black woman, a celebrity, and I'm out. It *was* a big deal. No regrets.

I grew up watching a lot of comedy. Our whole family would just sit there watching TV and laugh. One who really stayed with me was Jackie "Moms" Mabley. She was the first black woman that I saw doing stand-up. My comedy has to come from a real place so it would be hard for me not to talk about my sexuality. In a lot of them I talk about my wife and my kids. What's funny is that I would get off stage and someone would say, "You know, um, I really thought you were hilarious and all but you didn't really make a statement for, for gay rights." Like, jackass, I just did a whole fucking hour about my wife and kids! You can't get any gayer than that, what the fuck? You know. My life says it. My life is a speech for equality, and a speech for, hey, we all going through the same problems. Different sex, but same shit, same problems.

Wanda Sykes

wazina
ZONDON

teacher

Wazina Zondon

Around six or seven, my parents told me about heaven and hell. And in that same breath, they said, "You're not allowed to have a boyfriend. When the time comes, we'll pick the man for you. We'll introduce you to him."

New York City, September 2012

I think I was like 14 when I came out to myself. I'm queer. I'm gay. That's sort of the way that I think straight people just know they're straight. It was like, "Oh." That's what I acknowledge.

I think it's important for us to reclaim words. "Queer" is one of those words that's traditionally been used in a really negative and derogatory way. It pushes me to think outside of the binary. There aren't just female and male. There is so much more diversity in each being. I was part of the Riot Grrrl scene - proud, feminist, punk, lesbian women. We were rejecting what it meant to be a woman. We were rejecting what it mean to be brown, what it meant to be yellow, what it meant to be all these other labels. I can shed misogyny, I can shed heteronormativity. It was a very welcoming space.

I went away to college in 2000. I never said to my parents, "I'm not coming back." But, it's not a reality in my family, it's not a reality in my culture, for a woman to not live at home. You leave home when you go to the next man's home, which is your husband. But in the end, I had to be really honest about all the things I wasn't telling them about. I wasn't telling them about my relationship, I wasn't really explicit about my sexual orientation.

And so, I wrote my parents a nine-page letter. I went home to visit my parents one weekend. My dad said, "Come with me to the supermarket. You should help me buy

A nd my parents did their best to straddle both cultures, American and Afghan. In the summers, we'd go to mosque and learn to read the Quran. We spoke Farsi or Dadi at home. But also we did things like ballet and soccer and block parties and those sorts of things.

Being queer or being gay or lesbian was never an option in our family. But I do remember seeing men and women at family functions dancing together. Men danced with men, women danced with women. I wondered if I could get away with being queer under the guise of, "We're just a very homo-social culture. I should have girlfriends."

groceries." And in the car, he did that thing where you turn off the radio. And he says, "I got your letter. I haven't shown it to your mom and I'm not going to. We're going to figure this out together. You're already a double minority. You're a woman in this country. You're an Afghan. You come from refugee parents. You don't have to prove anything. Don't live this life of struggle. There's no such thing as gay Afghans. So, if you think you're a lesbian, there's no such thing. But if you want to come out about it, just know I will not be able to be buried in Afghanistan." To think about jeopardizing his integrity, his dignity, and his honor is a frightening and a very shameful, upsetting place to be. But I also know where my resilience comes from—from that same man and from that same woman.

We never talked about sex or sexuality, which is exactly why I'm a sex educator now. I'm out to all my students. I think it offers young people so much to have visible LGBT adults and teachers in their school. It offers a young person the idea that, "I can make it. I can be an adult. I can be successful. If you did it, I can do it, too." That will do so much for a young person. And that does so much for what that young person can offer our world.

WE NEVER TALKED ABOUT SEX OR SEXUALITY, WHICH IS EXACTLY WHY I'M A SEX EDUCATOR NOW. I'M OUT TO ALL MY STUDENTS.

Wazina Zondon

jake
SHEARS

musician

Jake Shears

Part of me does feel happier that gay culture is kind of normalizing and then, the other side, it makes me sad a little bit too. I'm not gonna lie. There's something I love so much about being a homo. And I feel like anybody who's gonna be wagging their finger at us, it's like, you know, "Fuck, who cares? Fuck off."

New York City, October 2011

I would go see a band called The Cramps. The singer's name was Lux Interior. And he would come out in a black rubber smock, and lady slacks, and pumps—not too high—and totally just freak the fuck out, blow-jobbing the microphone. I don't know if he was ever gay or not, but he was the queerest thing I had ever seen. But that energy was what I wanted to give on stage.

The first few years, all the media was always calling us a gay band. It used to really dishearten me because, growing up, there'd be, like, "The Christian Cyndi Lauper." Or, "The Christian George Michael." Always being called a gay band was felt like the gay version of something real. I don't feel that way anymore. The last couple years, I started really writing music about being gay, my take on gay life in the past and the present.

People like Freddie Mercury, Elton John in those early years, George Michael, they were still having to hold in the person that

was watching *The Muppet Show* with my two sisters and Christopher Reeve was the guest host. He was so beautiful, I turned to my sisters and I said, "When I grow up, I'm going to marry him." And they proceeded to tell me that wasn't possible, that men can't marry men.

In my freshman year of high school, I shoplifted a *Playgirl* from the B. Dalton. I mean, it's so crazy that I took that risk, and it was a major, major risk. I didn't know what to do with this *Playgirl*. I couldn't just throw it in the garbage because somebody might come across it. So, I took it down to the water and I had to burn it. It was a very strange, kind of symbolic moment that I had to go down and burn the evidence.

they really were. I just think that would be so miserable. I can't imagine going out on stage and be shakin' around and doin' my high kicks, you know, and givin' some skin—I don't know how I could do it and at the same time not talk about my sexuality.

The year that I came out, there were these phone lines that you would call, and there were these chat rooms. Every once in a while, we'd have little parties where we would all get up and get together and meet each other, and you'd see these people that you were talkin' to on the phone. It was really a freak show. Talk about outsiders. I mean, these were proper outsiders. But it kinda felt like . . . a family.

I met this woman on this chat line, and we talked a lot on the phone, and we started becoming friends. She was really obese, and she had a problem getting around. She had a problem being in public. People would make fun of her. And so, we made this pact that if I ever made any money, I would get her gastrointestinal bypass surgery. So, I started making music and wrote this song for her called "Mary." Her name was Mary. We got the surgery for hwer, and it ended up killing her. She was probably the most important person in my life, as far as a friend.

Being on the outside gives you an incredible perspective and changes you as a person. It makes you have different ideas about what you see. I wouldn't give that up for the world.

BEING ON THE OUTSIDE GIVES YOU AN INCREDIBLE PERSPECTIVE AND CHANGES YOU AS A PERSON. IT MAKES YOU HAVE DIFFERENT IDEAS ABOUT WHAT YOU SEE. I WOULDN'T GIVE THAT UP FOR THE WORLD.

Jake Shears

ellen
DEGENERES

tv personality/actor

Ellen Degeneres

I don't want to be on television just to talk to the Kardashians. They're lovely people, but I'd like to actually make a difference while I'm here. I have a forum where I can actually say things that are important. My hope for the future is . . . that those low-rise jeans go out of style. Someone's gotta put an end to that. 'Cause when you bend over, your ass is hanging out. And that's not right.

Los Angeles, April 2011

When I was doing stand-up, I was traveling around in a lot of small towns, in a lot of cities where I wouldn't have been accepted at all as a gay comedian. As my career progressed and I was on television, then, certainly, I couldn't come out. You have all these people around you that help you stay closeted, because they're making money off of you. As long as they know, you get the sense that the world doesn't have to know. You say to yourself, "I'm not really closeted, I'm out. I'm just not out to the world and it's nobody's business." And you can justify that all you want, but the reality is, you're still a slave to it. And it's a heaviness that you live with inside. There's a fear that someone's not gonna like you because of this thing.

When I realized that I couldn't keep that secret anymore, I decided I would come out and my character would come out on the show. And I was celebrated for a short time and it was a big deal. And then, it was a horrible deal. I lost my show and I lost my career and I lost a lot. But I was able to be completely free.

It's just amazing to me that kids grow up around other gays kids now. I always felt like I was different. I just didn't know that I was different in the way that I was gay. I was a girl who didn't really like to wear dresses. And I was different because I was a girl who was not like other girls. I dated guys and I thought I'd kinda have to settle, 'cause I couldn't find somebody that I really, really thought I could be with for the rest of my life.

On my wedding day, I was feeling happier than I've ever been in my entire life. And, I'm marrying someone. I'm getting married. I'm not civil union-ing anybody. I'm very much a family person.

Ellen Degeneres

I like the idea of a home and a partner. Growing up, I never thought that I would ever meet somebody that would impress me as much as she impresses me, keep me excited and stimulated and laughing and learning. We have this amazing connection that I never thought I'd find with anybody.

The more that we have gay people who speak up, the more that we have gay people seen in positions of power, it impresses upon those who are just ignorant to the fact that gay people are out there. It helps them to realize, "Oh, I know someone who's gay." It's important, for this reason, that we are more visible.

After I came out, Matthew Shepard was killed. It was one of the most devastating things. Who knows who we lost, you know? For me, being someone who was famous and known, I thought, somehow, that my coming out would make a difference. It would help shift people's opinions. There are sensitive, little souls out there that are often up against some loud bullies. And we need to stop those loud bullies.

We need everybody. We need athletes and we need artistic people. We need quiet people, we need shy people, we need weird people. Some people get picked on 'cause they're too good-looking. I know that. I want it to be a gentler world. It's harsh and it's hard and it's cruel sometimes. And, well, I want it to be a better world.

THE MORE THAT WE HAVE GAY PEOPLE WHO SPEAK UP, THE MORE THAT WE HAVE GAY PEOPLE SEEN IN POSITIONS OF POWER, IT IMPRESSES UPON THOSE WHO ARE JUST IGNORANT TO THE FACT THAT GAY PEOPLE ARE OUT THERE.

Ellen Degeneres

suze
ORMAN

Suze Orman

I grew up on the South Side of Chicago—inner city, the hood. I had a speech impediment. I couldn't pronounce my R's, S's, or T's. I knew I was stupid. I knew I would never be anything. The entire class knew that. So, I never, ever really tried.

New York City, October 2012

was a waitress for *seven* years, making $400 a month. So, I go to interview for another job. This was 1980 and affirmative action was in full bloom. They didn't have any women stockbrokers at the time. Now, I'm not somebody who wears dresses or skirts. I don't feel comfortable in them. So, I get dressed in my red-and-white Sassoon pants, tucked into my white cowboy boots, with this blue silk shirt (are y'all gettin' the picture?), and go into Merrill Lynch.

Nobody knows what to do with me, and before I know it, I'm in the manager's office. Here I am now—a stockbroker at Merrill Lynch. And I'll never forget the first time that I'm sitting in a sales meeting, and it's all these male brokers and me. And the manager is up there saying, "Men, I want you to listen to me. The first time you ever sell a private, limited partnership, it will be better than the first time that you . . ." And I looked at him and I said, "Were you going to say, 'the first time you "hmmm" a woman?'" And he said, "Yeah." And I go, "I get that. I get that." By not judging them, they didn't judge me.

I've been a very responsible financial person. I have been able to acquire a serious sum of money. But here is what's

IF WE COULD BE LEGALLY MARRIED ON A FEDERAL LEVEL, ANY MONEY A SPOUSE LEAVES TO ANOTHER SPOUSE, IT COULD BE $10 BILLION, THEY CAN LEAVE IT TO EACH OTHER ESTATE TAX-FREE. THAT'S HOW IT WORKS FOR HETEROSEXUALS.

Suze Orman

going to happen: Upon my death, any money that I leave to KT, the love of my life, that is above the estate tax limit, she's going to lose—essentially half of all the money that I'm leaving to her, and I'm gonna lose whatever she leaves to me. If we could be legally married on a federal level, any money a spouse leaves to another spouse, it could be $10 billion, they can leave it to each other estate tax-free. That's how it works for heterosexuals.

And it's not just about estate tax. I was in Chicago giving a talk to 5,000 women and I'm not feeling good. On our way to the hospital, KT's saying to me, "Who am I going to tell them I am? I know, I'll tell them I'm your sister." "No, KT. You're gonna tell them you're my spouse." And she says, "No, Suze, I'm afraid. I'm afraid if I tell them that, they won't let me in." Really? We have to lie to be at the sides of the ones we love? At the time that KT has seen me suffer, that she should feel like she can't just be there as who she is, and she has to pretend that she's somebody she's not? It's just so wrong.

We spent many years in South Africa, a country that's gone through apartheid, that's oppressed more people maybe than anybody. Gay marriage is legal. In fact, it's so legal that there's really no difference at all between gay marriage, straight marriage, any of it. Where is it honored? Everywhere in the world, Suze, except the United States of America. And I'm like, "Are you kidding me? Are you kidding me?"

So, KT and I were married legally in South Africa. I hold up that marriage certificate every once in a while and I look at it. And I think to myself, maybe, just maybe, one day, we're gonna be able to get married, on a federal level, again. 'Cause what a heartbreak. South Africa recognizes me, but the United States of America doesn't. What does that say?

WE SPENT MANY YEARS IN SOUTH AFRICA,
A COUNTRY THAT'S GONE THROUGH
APARTHEID, THAT'S OPPRESSED MORE
PEOPLE MAYBE THAN ANYBODY. GAY
MARRIAGE IS LEGAL. IN FACT, IT'S SO LEGAL
THAT THERE'S REALLY NO DIFFERENCE AT
ALL BETWEEN GAY MARRIAGE, STRAIGHT
MARRIAGE, ANY OF IT.

Suze Orman

twiggy pucci
GARCON

ballroom gatekeeper

Twiggy Pucci Garcon

There was always a feminine side to me. I was pulled into someone's office at my church and this someone said to me that if I didn't change how I was, I would be asked to leave. God loves all, but you are telling me that because I'm this way, I can't be here? That didn't click in my mind. It still doesn't make sense to me.

New York City, October 2012

've been a part of the mainstream ballroom scene since 2004. I was 14. The ballroom scene started around 1880. It later evolved around 1960-something, when the Harlem drag ball circuit arose. *Paris Is Burning* was definitely an epic film for our community. People started to understand what is a ball, what are the categories, what happens there, what is a house?

A house is called a house because it takes on the structure of a family. The structure of it is kinda the same, but with no respect to gender. I'm a man who is attracted to men, so I consider myself gay. But someone who is a post-op trans woman has a vagina, so she considers herself a woman who's attracted to men, which technically is heterosexual. So, it really is how you choose to identify yourself.

I have a butch queen mother, a femme queen mother, and a butch queen father. A butch queen mother can give me a very one-on-one, "You're a butch queen, I'm a butch queen," that kind of perspective of nurturing. A femme queen mother, on the other hand, is a female figure. It's a trans woman. So, that's a whole different type of advice that I get from her than from him. If you've been rejected by your biological family or you've been kicked out or shunned, whatever the case may be, and you have this surrogate family that becomes your family, it's not just ballroom. Ballroom is a competition. But a house is more than just a competition—that house is a real family.

Many people don't know that ballroom is still alive and well. There are categories and subcategories. Take "realness," for example, which is how well you fit into a heterosexual society. There's "butch

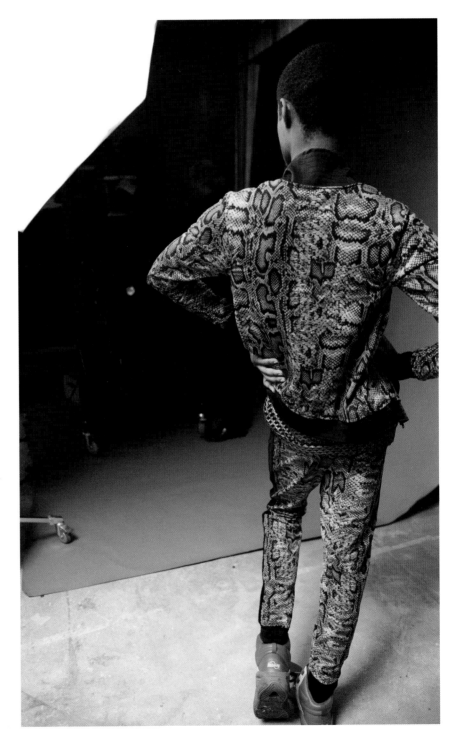

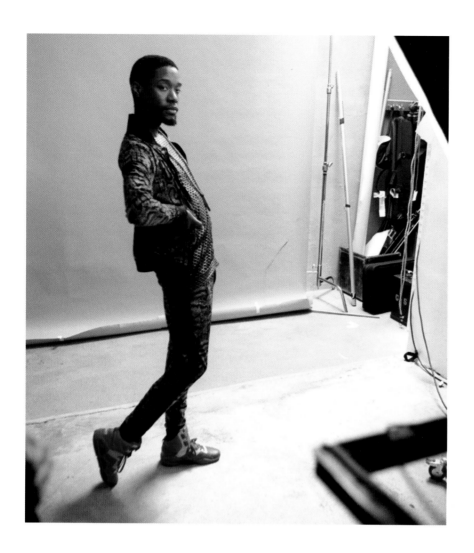

queen realness," which then breaks down into schoolboy, pretty boy, thug, executive. You also have "butch queen in drags realness," which is someone who lives his life as a man, but gets up in drags for the ball . . . and how much they look like a woman, that you wouldn't be able to say, "Oh my God, that's a man." Realness!

Being a part of the ballroom scene was nothing but a blessing. I don't think that creative aspect of my brain would've been as unlocked, had I not been in the ballroom scene. I wouldn't be as inspired to help people and make change. When I moved to New York in 2007, I thought it was to escape from Virginia, to go into the fashion industry and go to FIT and work Fashion Week and do this stuff. And in actuality, my purpose was to move up here to do what I'm doing now, to help the people who don't have anybody else to turn to.

FACES NY is the longest, minority-run, not-for-profit in Harlem that deals with the HIV and AIDS community. As a community health specialist, I do HIV testing and connection to treatment and care. That means I, myself, go with them to their first doctor's appointment. I, myself, go with them to make sure they get insurance.

I'm my mother's only child. I've had an honest conversation with her saying that either you accept me for all of who I am, or you get none of me. And my mother took all of me.

When I'm 30, Twiggy Pucci Garçon will be the same person, just with more life experiences. I'd probably have a restaurant, 'cause I love to cook. I'd be in a loving relationship, with children. I do want children. And, I'd still be helping people. That's never gonna change.

I'M MY MOTHER'S ONLY CHILD. I'VE HAD AN HONEST CONVERSATION WITH HER SAYING THAT EITHER YOU ACCEPT ME FOR ALL OF WHO I AM, OR YOU GET NONE OF ME. AND MY MOTHER TOOK ALL OF ME.

Twiggy Pucci Garcon

christine
QUINN

politician

Christine Quinn

I started working in New York City as a housing organizer. I met now-State Senator Tom Duane. He asked me to run his 1991 campaign to be the first openly gay City Council member and first openly HIV-positive elected official in the country. So, I took that job. And Tom would go around introducing me to everybody as his straight campaign manager, and he thought it was the funniest thing, that he had this straight campaign manager for this big, gay campaign.

New York City, March 2012

During the months running that campaign it became clear to me that this idea that I could be professionally successful, I could have friends, I could be happy, but I didn't need a romantic life and would never have one, was going be an untenable way to live. And I said to Tom, "I really need to talk to you about something important." And he said, "Oh my God, you're gonna quit." And I said, "No." And he said, "Oh, what are you a lesbian? Oh, we don't really have time for that. That's fine. Let's go."

I was the executive director of the New York City Gay and Lesbian Anti-Violence Project. And the thing I learned was you can actually work within a structure and push against that structure at the same time. For us at AVP, it was the police department. We would work with the police department, rewrite their training curriculums and we might, the next day after the training, organize a demonstration outside a precinct. If you disagree agreeably, you can work both inside and outside, and actually get things done, in a pretty broad way.

I don't really know why the Republicans are using such hideous and mean anti-gay rhetoric. The idea that you have to lift yourself up by pulling other people down, it's just not nice and I don't understand why you would want be on the international stage and behave in a way that your mother would have told you isn't nice. Your mother told you not to pick on people. I don't really understand that.

We can pretend words don't matter, but words do matter. Marriage is a word that is universally recognized. Everybody knows the literal definition of it and the societal definition of it. And if you say, "I can't get married," everybody knows what that means, too. It means the law is not with and for and about you. To say all these other families can have that, but you have to have this other thing that we had to create, that nobody heard of until we came up with it, and isn't as good as the real thing that's been around since they made dirt, you're left out.

Marriage passed in New York State after it failed. In 2009, there was a vote and we lost. And we lost badly. What was great about 2011 is we won with diverse support. We had a letter from business leaders—from Lloyd Blankfein, the head of Goldman Sachs. I don't think he was ever a Queer Nation member, you know what I'm saying? He signed a letter with other huge business leaders, asking the State Senate to do this.

Two days after marriage passed was the Pride Parade. I got to march with Governor Cuomo, and it was . . . you really weren't marching—you were kinda, like, floating down. I don't know that I've ever seen such unadulterated joy.

If you had asked people 10 years ago, "Would, in 2011, New York State pass marriage equality?" If you told them Massachusetts, Connecticut, all these other states passed it too, they would tell you that you were nuts. The truth is, we have succeeded beyond anything we could have dreamt of. You can't have that much success and not be energized and excited by it. And you're not allowed, really, to have that much success and to squander it. You have to harness it and use it.

THE IDEA THAT
YOU HAVE TO LIFT
YOURSELF UP BY
PULLING OTHER
PEOPLE DOWN, IT'S
JUST NOT NICE . . .

Christine Quinn

cynthia
NIXON

actress

Cynthia Nixon

There are a lot of people who really don't believe people when they say they're bisexual. So, I try and avoid the bisexual label because it just brings so much grief down on you. People think you're faking, you're wishy-washy. Or people think you're a sex addict or something, who doesn't want to make up their mind. I want be a political fighter and I want to be in there fighting, so I call myself gay. And certainly, I'm delighted to be in the gay club.

New York City, January 2013

Marriage equality is so much the right issue for me to kinda pin my hat on. Because, after years of being in love with a man and everybody badgering us to get married, all of a sudden, I was in love with a woman whom I actually wanted to marry, and I wasn't allowed to.

In a society where there are two different sets of rules for different kinds of people, you're immediately sending a message that those people, who don't have those rights, are somehow lesser. That they're not really full citizens and they're not maybe even really human. You're sending a message to the worst elements in society: "If you want find someone to pick on, this is a good group, because the government's not going to protect them."

Being out, how will that affect being cast in things? It's very difficult to gauge. You don't really know about the parts you didn't get cast in. I was offered three roles in a row just now that were all lesbian roles. My daughter, who's 16, was saying to me, "How do you feel about that? Do you feel like, all of a sudden, you're now being typecast?"

My daughter is Jewish and she's being raised Jewish. And I was thinking it's very similar to being a Jewish performer. You can complain, "Why do I always get the Jewish roles?" But so much better that you get the Jewish roles and they have a Jew actually playing the Jewish character rather than A) there are no Jewish roles or

People all the time talk about "When I came out." Well, I don't feel like I came out. I feel like I fell in love with someone, and that person was a woman. I don't want to minimize that in any way. What I'm attracted to about Christine is her butchness and her gayness. But I don't feel like, all of a sudden, there was a part of me that had been, you know, denied or living in the shadows, that finally could come out.

Gay people are fighting really, really hard for our civil rights. What's important is the world looks at all of us and sees us as gay. And so, we need to be cohesive and we need to fight as one community.

B) they get some Irish person who doesn't know anything about being Jewish. We've got to embrace those roles and we've got to play those roles.

Now that Christine and I are married, there is a way that people see us and treat us that is different. Somehow, we are understood as a family in a way that we hadn't been before.

I am not a particularly religious person, but I am somewhat religious. The left in general have made a terrible mistake ceding religiosity to the right. Bishop Gene Robinson, who performed Christine and my wedding ceremony, said, "When America was founded and we said, 'we,' we had a very particular bunch of people we were talking about: white, male property holders."

And gradually, the "we" became larger and larger. So then, it was white men and black men who had been freed by that point. And then, gradually, it was opened up to include women. Gay people are . . . are kind of the, almost the final frontier. This is what the gay rights movement is about, saying that I, as a gay person, am part of "we." It can't be "us and them" anymore. We have to understand, we're all "us."

PEOPLE ALL THE TIME TALK ABOUT "WHEN I CAME OUT." WELL, I DON'T FEEL LIKE I CAME OUT. I FEEL LIKE I FELL IN LOVE WITH SOMEONE, AND THAT PERSON WAS A WOMAN.

Cynthia Nixon

biographies

Christine Quinn is a Democratic politician and the first female and first openly gay Speaker of the New York City Council. She began her career in politics as the campaign manager and chief of staff for Thomas Duane, the first openly gay city council member in New York and first HIV-positive person elected to office.

Cynthia Nixon is best known for her portrayal of Miranda in the HBO series *Sex and the City*. She has received two Screen Actors Guild Awards, two Emmy Awards, a Tony Award, a Grammy Award, and a GLAAD Media Award. She is a graduate of Barnard College.

Dustin Lance Black is a screenwriter, producer, director, and social activist. He won the Academy Award and two WGA Awards for *Milk*, the biopic of the late civil rights activist Harvey Milk. He is also a founding board member of the American Foundation for Equal Rights (AFER), which is leading the Federal Case against Prop 8.

Ellen DeGeneres is a stand-up comedian, actress, and the host of *The Ellen DeGeneres Show*. She has won twenty Emmy Awards and has been included in Forbes 100 Most Powerful Women and *Entertainment Weekly*'s 50 Most Powerful Entertainers. She is married to actress Portia de Rossi.

Jake Shears is the lead male vocalist of Scissor Sisters. The band has been nominated for a Grammy and collaborated with a wide range of artists such as Elton John and Kylie Minogue.

Janet Mock is a writer, a transgender rights advocate, and the former staff editor of *People* magazine's website. She now creates transgender-specific programs and education for the LGBTQ youth center of the Hetrick-Martin Institute.

Lady Bunny is a promoter, DJ, and legendary drag queen. She is a founder of Wigstock and currently serves as the Dean of Drag on the TV series *RuPaul's Drag U*.

Larry Kramer is the co-founder of two groundbreaking LGBT organizations, Gay Men's Health Crisis and ACT UP. A respected playwright and author, he has received two Obies, a Tony Award, an Academy Award nomination, and was a finalist for the Pulitzer Prize.

Lupe Valdez is the first female, Latina, and lesbian sheriff of Dallas County, Texas. Prior to her thirty-year career in law enforcement, she was a captain in the United States Army.

Neil Patrick Harris currently stars in the TV show *How I Met Your Mother*, for which he won an Emmy. He was named one of *Time* magazine's 100 Most Influential People in 2010 and has two children with his partner David Burtka.

R. Clark Cooper is the former executive director of Log Cabin Republicans. He received several appointments in the George W. Bush administration and served in Iraq as an officer in the United States Army Reserve.

Suze Orman is a financial advisor and the host of *The Suze Orman Show*. She is a *New York Times* best-selling author and *Forbes* recently named her one of the Top 10 Most Influential Celebrities.

Twiggy Pucci Garcon is a ballroom performer and founder of the Kiki scene's House of Pucci. He is a community health specialist at FACES NY, the oldest minority-run HIV & AIDS non-profit in Harlem.

Wade Davis is a former professional football player and NFL Europe Champion. He is the assistant director of job readiness at the Hetrick-Martin Institute in New York.

Wanda Sykes is a stand-up comedian and actress. She's won an Emmy, an American Comedy Award, and been named one of the 25 Funniest People in America by *Entertainment Weekly*.

Wazina Zondon is a Muslim-identified Afghan woman. She teaches sex education and speaks about the intersection of homophobia and Islamaphobia.

AFTERWORD

We started our company, D&P Creative Strategies, LLC to effect social change through media. In 2009 when we viewed *The Black List* documentary, we were compelled to figure out how to replicate these poignant African American stories with Latino voices. We then persuaded the amazing Timothy Greenfield-Sanders, Michael Sloane, and Tommy Walker, producers of *The Black List*, to work with us to produce a doc about the perseverance, hard work, and achievement of Latinos and Latinas in America.

It was a life-altering experience to harness the talent of exceptional Latino and Latina leaders and produce two volumes of *The Latino List*, helping change attitudes toward our community. As Latina lesbians we were equally passionate about telling the stories of our LGBT brothers and sisters and were thrilled to once again work with Timothy and his team including: Michael Sloane, Tommy Walker, Sam McConnell, Orlan Boston, Wesley Adams, and Chad Thompson on *The Out List*.

The List film series has come at pivotal and historic moments in our nation's history. *The Black List* was released during the ascendency of the nation's first African American president. The film turned the very notion of being "blacklisted" on its head, from a term of disenfranchisement to one of distinction and pride. *The Latino List* coincided with the introduction of Arizona SB-1070, during the height of hateful speech spewing from various media outlets about Latinos in America. We viewed the creation of this documentary as an opportunity through storytelling to share the rich and vibrant history of patriotism and pride in what America has given our families and what we offer back. Our goals were threefold: to touch hearts and minds, help transform them, and provide role models to young children all across America.

The Out List comes at yet another critical time in our history. The United States Supreme Court, has heard two same-sex marriage cases, making it the first time that the freedom for same-sex couples to marry has been considered by the nation's highest court.

We were honored to be guests of our friend and Associate Justice of the Supreme Court Sonia Sotomayor (featured in *The Latino List: Volume 1*) at *Windsor v. United States*, challenging the Defense of Marriage Act, which prohibits federal marriage benefits for legal marriages between same-sex couples. No *words* can adequately describe how it felt to bear witness to the oral arguments that would determine our fate and the fate of millions of gay, lesbian, bisexual, and transgender couples like us to be able to marry the person we love and enjoy the same federal benefits as our straight brothers and sisters.

Every time we have the audacity to share our intimate story and educate someone about what it means to be gay in America, we change hearts and minds. Through this film and book we are sharing personal and often private stories of heroism. We want what everyone in America wants: to live a life without discrimination. As civil rights leader Cesar Chavez said:

Once social change begins, it cannot be reversed. You cannot un-educate the person who has learned to read. You cannot humiliate the person who feels pride. You cannot oppress the people who are not afraid anymore.

—Ingrid Duran & Catherine Pino

ACKNOWLEDGEMENTS

Over the past five years, in collaboration with HBO documentary films, I have directed and produced three films on African Americans followed by two on Latinos. One would think that *The Out List* was "an inevitability," but oddly enough it took the shocking passage of California's Proposition 8, on the night of Obama's historic election in 2008, to really jolt us into action. We'd all been thinking about a way, in film, to profile gay achievement, but Prop 8 brought much needed focus to the idea.

At first we called the project "Generation 8." It was to be an examination of LGBT rights in the post-Prop 8 world. California's hideous new law was a turning point for the gay rights movement, a Stonewall for a new generation. But we quickly realized that Prop 8 had angered people beyond those fighting for marriage equality. Activists across the country were galvanized to end Prop 8, but also wanted to speak to a range of LGBT discrimination issues.

In my mind, pre-production officially started on September 9, 2010, when my longtime friend Fern Mallis dragged me to a last-minute fashion show at Lincoln Center. I found myself next to Ellen DeGeneres with thirty seconds to pitch her the film. "Sounds great, send me something," she said.

Six months later, Ingrid Duran, Catherine Pino, Orlan Boston, Tommy Walker, Charlie Smith, Sam McConnell, and I were on a Burbank sound stage with Ellen sitting in front of our cameras. I vividly remember that just seconds before the interview started Ellen asked, "Now, who else has sat for this film again?" Sheepishly, we explained that she was the first. She was not fazed. And so, enormous gratitude goes to Ellen DeGeneres for believing in us early on. I'd like to also thank Ellen's wonderful team and especially Caryn Weingarten and Craig Peralta for their terrific help and support.

The Out List team formed organically. Longtime friend, photographer Roger Moenks insisted I meet Orlan Boston, then partner and chief diversity officer at a global management consulting firm. Orlan is now a partner at a Big 4 consulting firm where he leads a national Life Sciences and Healthcare M&A practice. In addition, Orlan brought us Wesley Adams, COO of Purpose Foundation, an incubator for new social movements. Wes has helped us better understand new media and social networking. Both Orlan and Wes gave so much of their time and energy.

Veteran *The Latino List* executive producers and owners of D&P Creative Strategies, Ingrid Duran and Catherine Pino, wanted this film to happen as much as they did *The Latino List*. Ingrid and Catherine were, as usual, terrific to work with.

Chad Thompson, founder of communa-k inc., is a fashion, branding, and publicity expert. Chad co-produced my last film, *About Face*, and was equally enthusiastic this time around. No one can wrangle a celebrity like Chad Thompson!

Tommy Walker is an integral and core member of our team. Starting in 2006, Tommy has helped produce all *The Black List* and *The Latino List* films. He's unstoppable and unflappable.

Michael Slap Sloane is another long-time "list" project producer. Michael's advice and counsel are highly regarded by all of us.

Special thanks go to art director, Aaron Eiseman, for our visual identity; project friend, Corey Johnson, for some key introductions; and *Latino List* book editor, Erasmo Guerra, for connecting us to Obama inaugural poet, Richard Blanco.

We are all enormously grateful to Richard for his spectacular, poignant, and poetic essay for this book. Thank you Richard, so very much.

The List Projects have achieved an unusually high level of visibility because of HBO and glorious support from my dear friends, Sheila Nevins and Lisa Heller. Their belief in me and their support for me as a film director and producer is impossible to overstate. Thank you Sheila and Lisa for all your love and dedication.

Lastly, I'd like to thank my great friend, Sam McConnell. Sam's thoughtful interviews brought out important truths from our sitters. His dedication to this film was an inspiration to me.

Thank you again Catherine, Chad, Ingrid, Michael, Orlan, Sam, Tommy, and Wesley.

—Timothy Greenfield-Sanders

Timothy Greenfield-Sanders with Suze Orman

Perfect Day Films Inc.
Timothy Greenfield-Sanders
c/o Iddo Arad
Frankfurt Kurnit Klein & Selz, PC
488 Madison Avenue 10th Floor
New York, NY 10022

Designed by Luxury Custom Publishing LLC
Library of Congress Cataloging-in-Publication Data available

ISBN: 978-0-9833033-7-4

Printed in Mexico
10 9 8 7 6 5 4 3 2 1

LCP LUXURY CUSTOM PUBLISHING
3920 Conde Street
San Diego, CA 92110
www.luxurycustompublishing.com